FOCUS ON MAMMALS

CLASSIFICATION

Stephen Savage

WAYLAND
www.waylandbooks.co.uk

This edition published in 2014 by Wayland
Copyright © Wayland 2014

Wayland
338 Euston Road
London NW1 3BH

Wayland Australia
Level 17/207 Kent Street
Sydney, NSW 2000

Editor: Carron Brown
Designer: Alyssa Peacock

Dewey number: 599-dc23

ISBN 978 0 7502 8076 1

Printed in China

10 9 8 7 6 5 4 3 2 1

Picture acknowledgements:
Bruce Coleman Inc. 4, /Andrew Purcell 5, /Jeff Foott Prod. 6, /Mark Boulton 7, /Jeff Foott Prod. 9(lower), /Peter Davey 10, /E. & P. Bauer 11(lower), /Steffan Widstrand 12 and title page (inset), /D. & M. Plage 13(top), /Bruce Coleman Inc.13(lower), /William Paton 14(lower), /Leonard Lee Rue 15 (top and title page, main pic) /E. & P. Bauer 15(lower), /Staffan Widstrand 17, /Jane Burton 20, /P. Van den Berg 21, /Eckart Pott 22(top), /John Cancalosi 26, /Sula Wesi 27; FLPA /Foto Natura cover (inset), /Gerard Lacz 8; NHPA /Roger Tidman 11(top), /Nigel Dennis 9(top) 14(top l.), 16 /Roger Tidman 14(top r.), /Stephen Datton 18(top), /A.N.T. 18(lower), /Norbert Wu 19, /Anthony Bannister 22(lower) and contents page; Shutterstock, cover picture, Tim Flach 12; Wayland Picture Library 24(both), 25.

First published in 1999 by Wayland

Wayland is a division of Hachette Children's Books, an Hachette UK company.
www.hachette.co.uk

Contents

What a difference!

Elephants look very different from shrews and pandas. However, they are all mammals and they share a number of features.

MAMMAL CHARACTERISTICS

- Mammals are warm-blooded.
- Most mammals' bodies are covered in fur or hair.
- All mammals have lungs to breathe air.
- Most baby mammals are fully formed when they are born.
- Mammal mothers feed their young on milk.

← The African elephant is the largest mammal living on land. It can be 3 metres (10 feet) tall and weigh up to 6 tonnes.

The tiny pygmy shrew is the smallest mammal. It is only 36 millimetres (1½ inches) long and weighs 1.5 grammes (0.05 ounces).

Some mammals are giants and others are small enough to sit in your hand. They may also be very different in shape and colour. The world's largest mammal is the blue whale. One of the rarest mammals is the giant panda, which eats only bamboo in its forest home in China.

Simple key to the Animal Kingdom

Invertebrates   Vertebrates

Worms   Spiders   Fish   Reptiles   Mammals

Snails   Insects Amphibians   Birds

Invertebrates are animals that do not have a backbone.
Vertebrates are animals that have a backbone.

Where mammals live

Mammals live in all the world's important habitats. They are found in forests, grasslands, deserts, mountains, polar regions, rivers and oceans.

↓ With their fish-like bodies, these spotted dolphins are able to live their entire lives in the sea.

⬆ A giraffe can feed on the higher leaves of trees because of its long neck and legs. It can also spot predators a long way off and run from danger.

Mammals have special features that help them to live in these very different habitats. Monkeys living in the tops of trees have hands to grip branches and a tail to help them to balance.

MAMMALS AND DIFFERENT HABITATS

- **Many tree-living mammals never go down to the ground.**
- **Some desert mammals do not have to drink water.**
- **Some mammals dig burrows to hide from danger.**
- **Mammals living in cold regions have thicker fur in the winter.**

Catching a meal

All mammals need food to live. However, the type of food and the way they eat can be very different.

↓ A tiger climbs down from rocks as it spots its prey.

AVOIDING DANGER

- Brown-coloured antelope are hard to see.
- Opossums pretend to be dead to escape danger.
- Armadillos have tough, leathery armour on their bodies.
- Porcupine spines are around 25 centimetres (10 inches) long.

↑ The aardvark lives in the African grasslands. It uses its sticky tongue to catch tiny termites for food.

Some mammals eat plants and others eat animals. Many use sharp teeth or claws to obtain their food.

↓ Humpback whales use their sieve-like mouths to strain tiny animals from the sea to eat.

A few mammals use tools to help them catch their food. They use sticks to prise out insects from holes, and break the hard shells of nuts, eggs or shellfish by banging them with rocks.

↓ A chimpanzee carefully pushes a twig into a termites' nest, then eats the termites that cling on to the end of the stick.

← Hedgehogs feed mainly on small animals and fruit. They curl into spiny balls if they sense danger.

Mammals that are hunted for prey often live together for safety. Some mammals have hard skin, prickly spines or foul smells to protect them against predators.

↓ A skunk defends itself against attack by squirting a foul-smelling liquid as far as 5 metres (16 feet).

Hot and cold

HOW TO KEEP WARM AND COOL

- Most mammals shiver to keep warm.
- Small baby mammals huddle together for warmth.
- Some mammals hibernate during the winter.
- Most mammals sweat to keep cool.
- Small desert mammals keep cool in their burrows.
- Elephants fan their ears to keep cool.

A mammal's fur or hair helps to keep it warm. In cold countries, mammals need very thick fur all year round.

The polar bear lives in the ➔ Arctic. It is the largest meat-eating mammal. Its thick white fur keeps it warm in the ice and snow.

Some mammals live in countries with hot and cold seasons. Their hair may be short in the summer and grow long and thick in the winter.

American bison grow a thick coat → of hair for the winter.

↓ Whales, the world's largest mammals, have no fur. This 8-m (26-foot) killer whale is covered in thick blubber, which keeps it warm even in cold parts of the oceans.

Small mammals shelter in their burrows to keep cool on very hot days. Larger mammals move to the cool shade of a tree. Tree-climbing mammals find shady branches to keep them cool.

↑ This squirrel lives in the scorching African desert. It uses its tail as a sunshade.

↓ A muddy pool is perfect for keeping a Cape buffalo cool on a hot day.

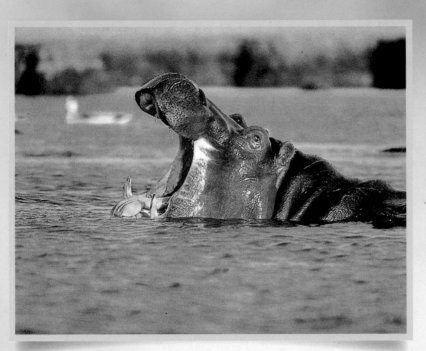

Bathing in a quiet stream or a mud pool, or having a dip in the sea, are good ways of staying cool.

← Hippos spend 18 hours a day in water to keep themselves cool.

↓ This Hawaiian monk seal keeps itself cool on a hot beach by going to sleep.

Getting around

Most mammals use all four legs when walking or running. They walk when travelling slowly and run to go faster. Kangaroos walk on all four legs but they use their back legs to make huge leaps when escaping from danger.

MOVING AROUND

- The cheetah is the fastest land mammal.
- The three-toed sloth is the slowest moving mammal.
- Dolphins swim and steer with their flippers and tail.
- Sea lions use flippers to walk and swim.

↓ When a Thomson gazelle runs at full speed, only a cheetah has a chance of catching it.

Mammals that climb trees have a tail that helps them to keep their balance. Kangaroos have tails to help them balance when they are bounding away from danger.

The three-toed → sloth lives in the South American rainforest. It grips tree trunks with its curved claws. It moves very slowly.

← Bats have large, leathery wings. These are formed from their very long front legs and toes.

Bats are the only mammals that can fly. However, there are several mammals that are able to glide through the air.

Sugar gliders live → in Australian forests. They have a flap of skin between their front and back legs, which helps them glide from one tree to another.

There are some mammals that swim in water only to catch food. Other mammals live in water all the time. They have a fish-like tail and flippers.

⬇ Sea lions use their front flippers like paddles for swimming. The back flipper is used for steering.

Mammal young

All newborn mammals are cared for by their parents. Some are born blind and helpless, while others can walk soon after birth. Mammal babies feed on their mothers' milk.

↑ Baby rabbits are born blind and helpless in the safety of their burrow.

Some types of mammals live in large groups. The young are still fed by their mothers, but they will be protected from danger by the whole group.

FACTS ABOUT YOUNG MAMMALS

* Baby monkeys cling to their mothers' fur.
* Baby dolphins are born in the sea.
* A newborn African elephant weighs 115 kilograms (254 pounds).
* Baby elephants need 34 litres (9 gallons) of milk a day.

↓ A newborn wildebeest can walk with its mother and the rest of the herd just 15 minutes after birth.

⬆ A lioness teaches her cubs what they will need to know to survive on their own.

Some mammals that live in groups, such as meerkats, share the care of the young. They may even have nurseries and babysitters.

⬅ A female meerkat will take care of the young of another female while she goes hunting.

Most mammals are fully formed at birth, but some change throughout their lives. A few females have babies that grow in a special pouch. Some, like the echidna, lay eggs.

↓ A baby kangaroo spends 300 days in its mother's pouch. Only one is born at a time.

Mammal pets

Look closely at pet mammals such as cats or dogs. You will see that in some ways they are quite similar to wild mammals such as tigers and wolves.

Rabbits can be kept in a hutch. ➤ There should be a dark section with straw so that it is like a wild rabbit's burrow.

⬇ Dogs are related to wolves, which live in a group. This is why dogs enjoy the company of humans.

HOW TO TAKE CARE OF YOUR PET MAMMAL

- Provide a cage or somewhere for it to sleep.
- Give it the right food and plenty of water.
- Remember all mammals need exercise.
- Keep the pet's cage clean.
- Most mammal pets enjoy company, so they shouldn't be left alone for long periods.

↓ Hamsters have a cheek pouch for storing food to eat later.

If your cat or dog has babies, you will see how mammal parents look after their young. You must not touch them or get too close.

Unusual mammals

Some mammals seem very strange. They appear to have extra features added or others missing. Mole rats, for instance, have no hair at all and never leave their underground tunnels, where they feed on plant roots.

↑ The Australian duck-billed platypus uses its large, flattened bill to pick up food from the bottom of rivers.

UNUSUAL FEATURES

* Very large eyes and ears for finding food at night.
* Webbed feet for swimming.
* Long arms for swinging through trees.
* A tail that acts like an extra hand.

Other mammals have extra-large features to help them live in difficult conditions. For instance, the elephant's trunk helps it to get water from deep underground.

But of all the mammals in the world, perhaps humans are the strangest.

Tarsiers have special toe pads for ➤ gripping branches. They hunt at night for insects and small animals.

Scale of mammals

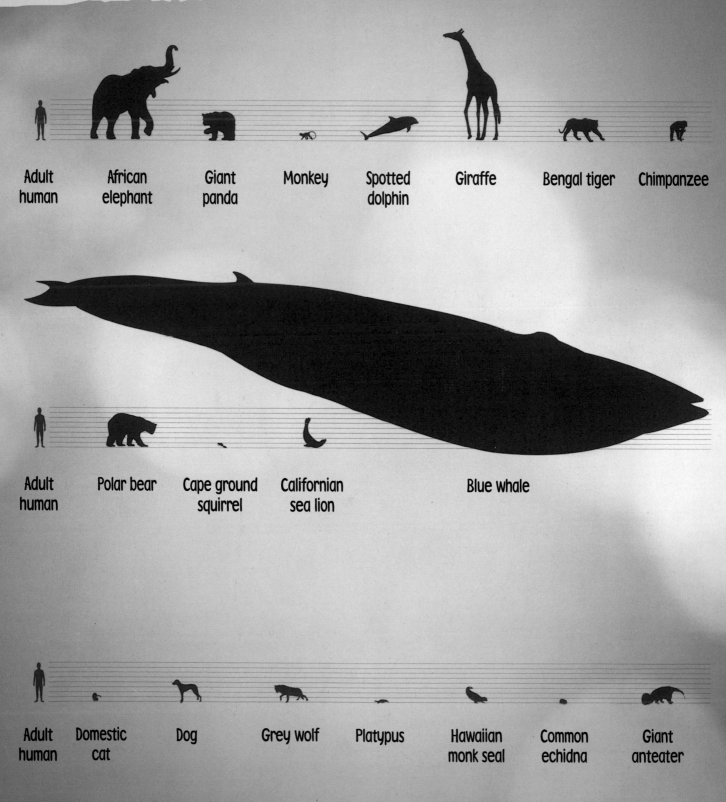

Adult human · African elephant · Giant panda · Monkey · Spotted dolphin · Giraffe · Bengal tiger · Chimpanzee

Adult human · Polar bear · Cape ground squirrel · Californian sea lion · Blue whale

Adult human · Domestic cat · Dog · Grey wolf · Platypus · Hawaiian monk seal · Common echidna · Giant anteater

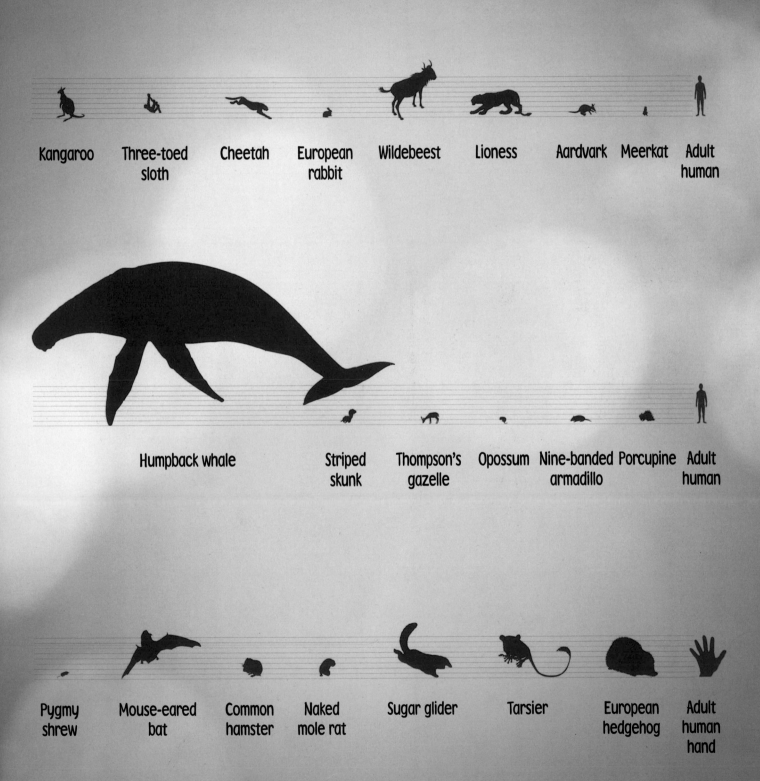

Kangaroo Three-toed sloth Cheetah European rabbit Wildebeest Lioness Aardvark Meerkat Adult human

Humpback whale Striped skunk Thompson's gazelle Opossum Nine-banded armadillo Porcupine Adult human

Pygmy shrew Mouse-eared bat Common hamster Naked mole rat Sugar glider Tarsier European hedgehog Adult human hand

Topic web

SCIENCE
Comparison of human features with features of other mammals.

How mammals adapt to their environment.

Food chain.

Growth and reproduction of mammals.

MATHS
Measurement and comparison of mammal sizes with each other and with humans.

GEOGRAPHY
Mammal habitats.

Position of different habitats on a world map.

ENGLISH
Write a diary entry - 'a day in the life of' a chosen mammal.

DRAMA/DANCE/MUSIC
Improvise to show movement of mammals.

Create music to illustrate mammal sounds.

ARTS & CRAFTS
Make a mural or collage showing a mammal or mammals and its/their habitat.

Design camouflage patterns.

Activities

Science Look at the similarities and differences between you and other mammals. What features are the same? What features are different? How do these features help mammals to survive? Make a chart showing a food chain.

Geography Look up the main deserts, rainforests and grasslands in an atlas. Draw a simple world map showing these habitats and which mammals live in them.

Arts & Crafts Use art materials to make a mural of different mammals. Use camouflage patterns to make a design.

English Choose a mammal and write a story about it. Where does it live? What does it eat? How does it move around? What dangers does it face?

Drama/Dance/Music Create a piece of drama or dance to show how different mammals move. Use music to help express the movement of different mammals. For example, deep, slow music for an elephant and fast, bouncy music for a kangaroo.

Maths Measure yourself with a tape measure. Then, using the scale on pages 28-29, draw a chart to show how many mammals are bigger than you and how many are smaller.

Glossary

Arctic The region at or around the North Pole.

Armadillo A small animal covered with bony plates like body armour. It lives in Central and South America.

Blubber The fat of whales and other sea mammals.

Burrows Holes dug in the ground by rabbits, foxes and other animals for shelter.

Camouflage Protection from attack by appearing to be part of the surroundings.

Habitat The natural home of a plant or animal.

Hibernate To spend the winter in an inactive state resembling sleep.

Invertebrates Animals that do not have a backbone or spine.

Opossum A tree-living marsupial.

Polar regions The areas around the North and South poles.

Predator An animal that hunts others for food.

Prey Animals that are hunted and killed for food.

Termites Ant-like insects living in large colonies.

Vertebrates Animals that have a spine or backbone.

Warm-blooded Refers to mammals whose body temperature stays about the same and is warmer than the surrounding air temperature. The skin may become hotter or colder, but the body temperature does not change.

Finding out more

Books to read

Mammal Kingdom – My Day at the Zoo by Terry Jennings (QED Publishing, 2011)

RSPB First Book of Mammals by Anita Ganeri, David Chandler and Mike Unwin (A & C Black Publishers Ltd, 2011)

Wildlife Wonders: Why Do Mammals Have Fur? by Pat Jacobs (Franklin Watts, 2014)

Nature Detective: British Mammals by Victoria Munson (Wayland, 2014)

Websites

Whale and Dolphin Conservation
www.wdcs.org/wdcskids/en/worldofwhales.php
Discover the world of whales and dolphins, including those that may swim in the sea near you.

Wildlife Watch
www.wildlifewatch.org.uk/explore-wildlife/animals/mammals
Check out this website to discover the large range of mammals that can be spotted in the UK.

Index

Page numbers in **bold** refer to photographs.